Items should be returned on or before the date shown below. Items
not already requested by other borrowers may be renewed in person,
in writing or by telephone. To renew, please quote the number on the
barcode label. To renew online a PIN is required. This can be requested
at your local library.
Renew online @ **www.dublincitypubliclibraries.ie**
Fines charged for overdue items will include postage incurred in recovery.
Damage to or loss of items will be charged to the borrower.

Leabharlanna Poiblí Chathair Bhaile Átha Cliath
Dublin City Public Libraries

Brainse Rinn Na Seád
Comhairle Cathrach
Ringsend Branch
Bhaile Átha Cliath
Dublin City Council

Tel 01 6680063

Due Date	Due Date	Due Date

Written by Guy Campbell
Illustrated by Simon Ecob
Edited by Rachel Carter and Imogen Williams
Designed by Barbara Ward
Cover design by John Bigwood
With thanks to Toby Buchan and Philippa Wingate

First published in Great Britain in 2018 by Buster Books,
an imprint of Michael O'Mara Books Limited,
9 Lion Yard, Tremadoc Road, London SW4 7NQ

 www.busterbooks.co.uk Buster Children's Books @BusterBooks

A CIP catalogue record for this book is available from the British Library.

ISBN: 978–1–78055–509–6

1 3 5 7 9 10 8 6 4 2

This book was printed in January 2018 by 1010 Printing International Ltd, 1010 Avenue, Xia Nan Industrial District, Yuan Zhou Town, Bo Luo County, Hui Zhou City, Guang Dong Province, China.

INTRODUCTION

This book explains all the skills you'll need to get through even the toughest day. You'll learn everything from basic survival techniques out in the wilderness, to skills you'll need when confronted by dangerous, bloodthirsty animals.

When you've read this book from start to finish, sign the certificate at the back of the book to show off your new know-how skills.

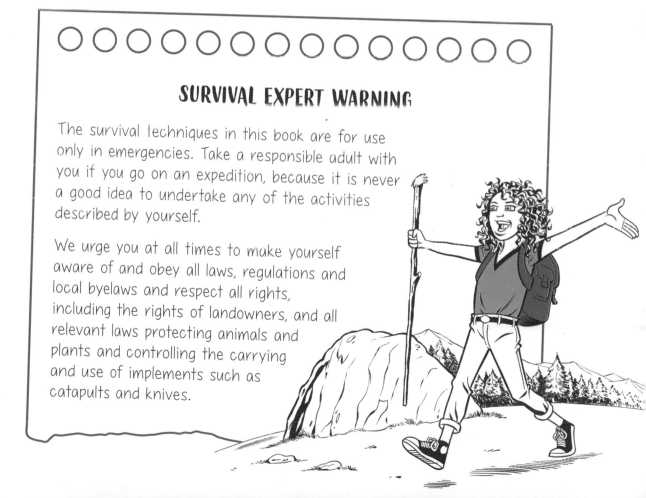

SURVIVAL EXPERT WARNING

The survival techniques in this book are for use only in emergencies. Take a responsible adult with you if you go on an expedition, because it is never a good idea to undertake any of the activities described by yourself.

We urge you at all times to make yourself aware of and obey all laws, regulations and local byelaws and respect all rights, including the rights of landowners, and all relevant laws protecting animals and plants and controlling the carrying and use of implements such as catapults and knives.

CONTENTS

HOW TO ...
PLAN A GROUP EXPEDITION

'Expedition' is the word used to describe a trip with a purpose. Here are some tips on how to make sure any expedition you and your team embark upon is well planned and goes without a hitch.

1 The first thing to do when planning an expedition is to come up with a 'mission statement'. This is a couple of sentences that clearly describe where you are going on the trip, why you are going, and what you want to achieve when you are away.

SAMPLE MISSION STATEMENT

"I plan to lead my team through the Atlas Mountains in Morocco. We will observe the hill tribes living there, and take some fantastic photos of the people and the landscape."

2 Use a map to plan your route to and from your destination. Work out how far your team can travel each day and plan where you will camp each night. Plan at least one alternative route both there and back in case you come across any obstacles on your journey.

3 Study books about previous expeditions to the area. Read and compare the accounts of at least three different people. Then make notes on the following points:

a) What type of weather you can expect? Decide on a start date and an end date for your expedition. Investigate the type of weather you can expect in the area at that time of year, as this will affect the clothing and camping equipment you will need to take.

b) What type of ground you will be covering? Is the terrain flat or mountainous? Do you need to take ropes and climbing gear, or would it be wiser to take cross-country skis?

c) Are there any natural sources of food or water along your planned route? How many days will you need to travel before you reach them? This will affect your calculations of how many days' food and drink rations you need to carry at the beginning of your journey.

d) Are there any deadly creatures you should watch out for along the way, such as snakes or poisonous spiders? This will influence the medical supplies you pack.

4 Make a list of everything that could go wrong on the expedition. What if someone fell ill from food poisoning or broke a leg? List the supplies and equipment you'd need in order to deal with each situation.

5 Match each member of your team with essential duties. These duties might include map-reading, shelter-building, monitoring rations, fetching water, cooking, gathering wood and building fires, keeping the camp clean, and watching out for dangerous animals.

6 Use all the information you have gathered to write up a 'trip plan'. Give a copy of the plan to everyone who will be going on the expedition. Leave a copy with someone who is not. This person can alert the emergency services if you do not return on time.

HOW TO ...
MAKE YOUR OWN SURVIVAL PACK

The equipment you take with you will depend on the type of expedition you are planning. But whether you are camping in the wilderness, hiking through mountains or trekking through a jungle, there are some expedition essentials that will keep you warm, dry and well fed.

ESSENTIAL ITEMS

- Water (as much as you can carry)
- Water purifying tablets
- Food rations (including high-energy food, such as chocolate and nuts)
- Maps
- A good compass
- Warm clothing (including a hat)
- Hiking boots
- A waterproof coat
- Camping equipment: tent, sleeping bag, cooking utensils
- A first-aid kit
- A whistle
- A flashlight (with spare bulb and batteries)
- A waterproof sheet (1.5 m by 2 m)
- Sturdy plastic bags for carrying water
- Wristwatch
- Fish hooks and twine
- Mobile phone
- Waterproof matches, a lighter and tinder
- Magnifying glass (which can be used to start a fire)
- A candle
- At least 8 m of cord
- Wire for making snares
- Insect repellent
- Sunscreen
- Emergency blanket
- A pocket knife with a selection of heads (legally, the blade must be non-locking, must fold away, and be no longer than 7.5 cm).

BEFORE YOU LEAVE

Check that all your electrical appliances are working and fully charged, or have new batteries before you set off.

Take a 'survival bag' with you. This is a large, brightly-coloured waterproof bag that you can sleep in if necessary.

Even if your expedition should only take you a couple of hours, pack the equipment and rations you would need to survive for at least 24 hours in an emergency.

BE A GOOD LEADER

You may find yourself with a group of people in a potentially dangerous situation, where someone needs to take the lead. Here are some things to remember if you step forward for the role of leader.

MAKE A STRONG START

- When you first meet the members of your team make eye contact with each of them. A confident, firm (but not too firm) handshake helps, too.

- Stand upright with your shoulders back. This will give your teammates confidence in your abilities. If you slouch you will look uninterested and nervous — not obvious leadership qualities.

- Try to remember everyone's name and repeat it back to them as you introduce yourself. People feel you're interested in them and will be more likely to trust you.

BE GOOD AT SOMETHING

If you read this book from cover to cover, your excellent survival knowledge will be sure to impress your team. Always make sure you have the right equipment for an expedition and, if all else fails, be witty and charming. Many leaders get to the top by putting people at ease and making them laugh.

ALWAYS TRY TO REMAIN POSITIVE

- Always look for solutions to the problems that you face rather than moaning about them. Complaining wastes time and can lower your team's spirits.

- Keep criticism to a minimum. If you are slow to blame people when things go wrong and quick to praise them if they perform a task well, your teammates will stay keen and cooperative.

- When one of your comrades is speaking to you, pay careful attention to what they are saying. Making use of your team's varied talents and expertise can only get you ahead.

CHOOSE A GOOD PLACE TO SHELTER

If you find yourself stranded in an unfamiliar environment, your top priority is to find a safe place to sleep. Well before darkness falls, you need to find a suitable place to shelter.

The most important thing a shelter provides is protection from the elements. In desert areas you will need to stay out of the sun. In mountains or polar regions rain, snow and wind will seriously threaten your chances of survival. Caves provide good natural shelter. Always check them out carefully first – you don't want to find you are sharing your new-found home with a surprised wild animal, such as a hibernating bear or a mountain lion.

Scout around for tell-tale signs that the cave may be occupied. These include bones, nests or droppings inside or near the cave entrance, and clumps of vegetation that are being used as bedding.

If you can't find a cave, look for a spot that is shielded from the elements. Camping at the base of rockfaces and cliffs will offer some shelter. However, check that there aren't any loose rocks lying around, as these would suggest you are in danger from falling debris.

THE IDEAL SPOT

A clearing in a wood is the ideal spot to make camp, especially if there is a fast-running stream near by. That way you will have building materials for your shelter, wood for your fire and water for drinking, washing and cooking.

PLACES TO AVOID

- Stay away from areas close to ponds or lakes. Water that isn't flowing attracts insects that might bite or sting you.

- Don't camp in a hollow at the bottom of a hill. Rain water may run off the hillside and flood your shelter.

- Avoid sheltering beside a cliff or rockface in snowy terrain, as this is where snow may build up and it could bury you while you sleep. There might also be a danger of avalanches.

- Never camp at the top of a hill as this will be exposed to the wind and rain. Your shelter could easily be blown away.

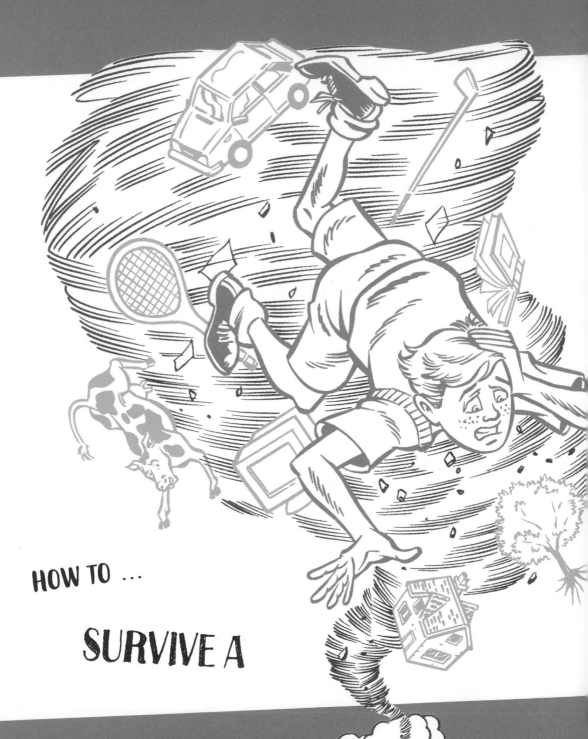

HOW TO ...

SURVIVE A

TORNADO

Tornadoes, also known as 'twisters', are wind storms that create a highly destructive, whirling funnel of air. They cause devastating damage to the areas they hit and happen very quickly, with little warning.

The best way to survive a tornado is to be prepared for it. If you live in an area that is prone to tornadoes, keep an eye on the weather by regularly logging on to a weather website, or tuning into TV or radio weather forecasts.

EARLY WARNING SIGNS

- Often you will hear a tornado coming before you see it. Listen out for a sound like a waterfall that turns into a roar as it gets closer. The sound of a tornado has been compared to that of a train or even a jet engine.

- The sky often turns a sickly greenish or greenish-black colour just before a storm hits.

- It may suddenly start to hail.

- You may notice clouds that are moving very fast, perhaps twisting into a cone shape.

- You might see debris, such as dust, branches and leaves, dropping from the sky.

- When the tornado arrives, you can expect to see a funnel-shaped cloud that is spinning rapidly. Debris will be pulled upwards into the funnel.

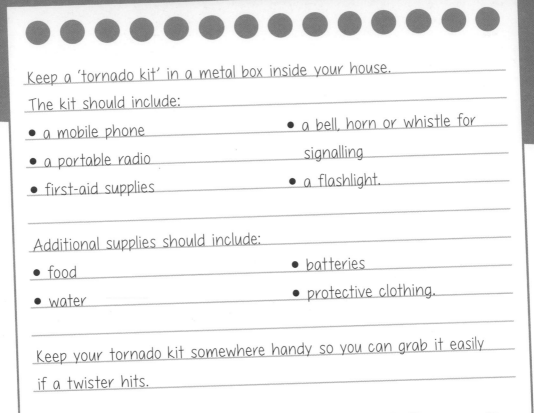

Keep a 'tornado kit' in a metal box inside your house.
The kit should include:

- a mobile phone
- a portable radio
- first-aid supplies

- a bell, horn or whistle for signalling
- a flashlight.

Additional supplies should include:

- food
- water

- batteries
- protective clothing.

Keep your tornado kit somewhere handy so you can grab it easily if a twister hits.

GET INSIDE

The best place to be when a tornado arrives is inside. Houses in areas that are prone to tornadoes often have 'storm cellars' underneath them. These are the safest places to hide. If the building you're in does not have a cellar, head for the lowest floor. Find the smallest room on that floor, such as a bathroom or cupboard. If that's not possible, look for a room in the middle of the house with no windows. A hallway may provide the best shelter.

Close any doors and windows that are located on the same side of the room as the approaching tornado. Open all the doors and

windows on the other side of the room. This will help prevent the powerful wind from entering the building. Tornadoes have been known to pick up entire buildings.

Take shelter under some solid furniture, such as a heavy kitchen table. If you are in a bathroom, jump into the bathtub. Cover yourself with a mattress, a sofa, towels or anything soft that you can get your hands on to protect yourself from flying debris.

SURVIVING OUTSIDE

If you are unlucky enough to be caught outside without buildings nearby, try to get out of the path of the tornado by moving to the side, rather than trying to outrun it.

Never hide behind a tree or climb into a car, caravan or tractor, as these may be sucked up by the tornado.

If the only shelter you can find is in a ditch or hollow, make sure you lie face down and use your arms to protect your head and neck.

SURVIVE FALLING OFF A HORSE

Horses have a habit of not doing quite what you want, and this occasionally includes dumping you on the ground. You are more likely to survive in one piece if you learn how to take a tumble.

1 Never mount your trusty steed without the right safety gear. A riding helmet could save your life. Wearing jeans and a tough long-sleeved jacket will protect your arms and legs from being scratched by low branches or being grazed if you fall on rough ground.

2 Once you have realized you are unfortunate enough to have chosen a horse that is impossible to control and that falling off is inevitable, try to look for a soft patch of ground to land on. It's better to fall off sooner on to sand, soil or grass rather than later on to rocks or gravel.

3 As you begin to fall, it is important to accept that you and your horse are going to part company for a while. Don't cling on for dear life. Kick your feet out of the stirrups and drop the reins to ensure that you aren't dragged cross-country.

4 As you fall, try not to tense up. Keep your limbs as floppy as possible. Resist the temptation to throw your arms straight out in front of you to break your fall. The only thing you will break is your bones. The more relaxed your body is, the better your landing will be.

5 As you fall, try to propel yourself as far away from your horse as you can to avoid being trampled under its hooves.

6 Ideally, you should attempt to land on your feet, bending your knees immediately on impact. Then curl into a ball and roll away from your horse to stop your vital organs hitting the ground. Cover your head and neck with your arms to protect your head.

7 Don't jump up as soon as you have rolled to a standstill. One by one test your fingers, arms, legs and especially your neck for damage by gently moving them. If everything seems intact get up very slowly. If you are injured, any sharp movements could make matters worse.

The good news is that you are in one piece. The bad news is that your horse is a long way away.

SURVIVE A DUEL

Imagine you wake up on a Monday morning and, instead of opening your eyes and seeing your messy bedroom, you find yourself transported back in time to the 17th century. Superb sword-fighting skills would be essential to your chances of survival.

WARNING

Never, ever pick up a real sword in the 21st century. Even in the 17th century, duelling was a last resort.

TOOLS OF THE TRADE

If you are right-handed, hold your sword in your right hand and vice versa if you are left-handed. Your sword is thin and whippy, so you shouldn't need to hold it with both hands.

THE 'EN GARDE' POSITION

Every musketeer knows the foundation of all good sword-fighting moves is a steady 'en garde' position. En garde allows the fighter to switch quickly between defending themselves or attacking their opponent.

1 Stand one large step away from being able to touch your opponent's outstretched sword with your own sword. Any closer and if your strike misses, you will be left standing in your enemy's strike range.

2 Turn your body to the side. Right-handers: point your right foot directly towards your opponent, keeping your left foot where it is (left-handers vice versa).

3 Bend your knees so that your body is well balanced.

4 Keeping your back as straight as possible, bend your sword arm at the elbow. Hold the handle (called the grip) of your sword level with your hips, with the point level with your head but slanting away from your body towards your enemy. This 'stance' will ensure your body is protected from your head to your hips.

5 Hold your other hand behind your back, or to one side, so it doesn't get in your way. You should feel well-balanced and comfortable in this position.

Make sure your back is to the sun — that way your enemy's body will be well lit, but yours will be hidden in shadow.

TACTICS

- As your opponent attempts to strike, straighten your arm and go in for the attack. Try to knock aside their sword with your own blade. Then quickly step forward and counter their strike with your own.

- Any strike is a good strike. Your opponent's legs, arms and even their hands are often easier to target than their torso.

- When fighting, conserve energy by keeping your movements to a minimum. Let your opponent do all the running around. They will soon tire.

- If you can, back them into furniture and make them fall over.

- When they are on the ground and swordless, you can afford to be chivalrous and let them leave unharmed.

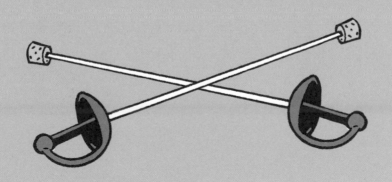

HOW TO ...
MAKE A
GETAWAY

You are on the run and need to put as much distance between yourself and your pursuers as possible. Here's how:

ON THE SCENT

If your pursuers are using tracker dogs, your chances of a clean getaway are smaller unless you can throw the dogs off your scent.

- Whenever possible stay downwind of the dogs so they can't pick up your scent on the air.

- Wade through water at every opportunity. This is the most effective way to leave no tracks and no scent.

- If you come to a stream, don't go straight across; it you have time, walk or swim up or down stream for a good distance before getting out on the other bank.

- Whenever possible, mingle with other people in a crowded place, so that your scent will be mixed with the scent of others.

- Best of all, if you can get yourself on a horse or a bicycle you will break your trail, and it will be very difficult for the nosy mutts to sniff you out.

DISGUISE YOUR TRACKS

Try not to leave an obvious trail. Stick to roads, rocks and other hard surfaces where you won't leave noticeable footprints. If you can't avoid leaving prints, don't waste a lot of time brushing them away. It is essential to move quickly, and brush marks are easy to spot.

'Backtracking' (walking backwards in your own tracks) is an excellent way to confuse trackers:

1 Find a starting spot that will make your trail harder to follow – such as a slab of stone or some shallow water.

2 Walk up to this spot, then walk backwards in your own tracks for ten paces.

3 Leap sideways off your trail and set off in a completely different direction. If the start of your new trail is hidden by a tree or bush, so much the better.

HOW TO …
SURVIVE AN ALIEN INVASION

No one is really sure what aliens look like. However, many people believe that they do exist and one day you might well come face-to-face with one.

JUST VISITING

If you're lucky enough to have bumped into an alien tourist it's a great opportunity to make extraterrestrial friends with it. Be as charming as possible, no matter how revolting it looks, and it may invite you to its home planet in return. Show it the sights – point out that Earth only has one sun, that it has one moon orbiting it, and that our sky is blue. Some planets have many moons and differently-coloured skies so be prepared for it to find this quite odd.

Be hospitable. You don't want the alien returning home to its planet, telling terrible stories about how horrible Earthlings are and then coming back with all its friends and family to either take over or destroy the Earth.

WORLD DOMINATION

Of course, if this alien is planning to take over the world it will not have much time for chit-chat. It will probably say something like: "Bow down inferior Earthling. You stand before the Emperor Zog. Prepare to meet your doom". In this case run like the wind and alert the authorities so they can declare a state of national emergency. If, however, your path is blocked by the spacecraft parked on your doorstep, try holding up a mirror in front of your extraterrestrial visitor. It will never have seen its reflection, so this is guaranteed to baffle it completely, and keep it busy until help arrives.

SURVIVE THE INVASION

Aliens usually start their invasions in capital cities because lots of powerful people work there. Gather together your friends and family and head away from the cities as soon as you hear of the invasion. Besides, fighting an alien invasion is best left to the professionals.

Take a radio with you so you can keep up to date with the latest alien movements and listen out for the all-clear.

Choose a place to hide that is as remote as possible so that you can stay out of the invaders' way.

All you need to do now is wait for Earth's armed forces to win the day, or for the aliens to get tired of the Earth's changeable weather and go home. Aliens do not like the rain and will do their utmost to avoid a shower. A few good thunderstorms should send them packing.

TOP TIP

Aliens might try to pose as humans. So look out for unusual behaviour in your loved ones. Avoid people with glowing eyes or weird-sounding voices — anyone showing confusion when performing simple human tasks, such as opening doors and putting on clothes, is also a dead giveaway.

HOW TO ...
MAKE A LADDER

Here's a quick and easy way of making a ladder. The type of knot you need to use is called a 'man-harness hitch'. You will need two equal lengths of sturdy rope and several short but tough lengths of a branch.

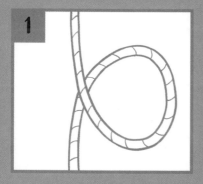

1

Put a loop in one rope.

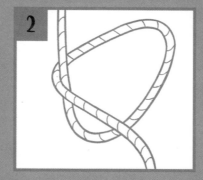

2

The bottom of the rope crosses over the loop as shown here.

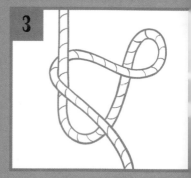

3

Put a twist in the top of the loop.

4

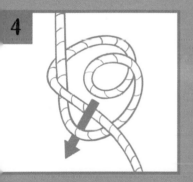

Take the twist over
the bottom of the rope
and tuck it through the
bottom of your loop.

5

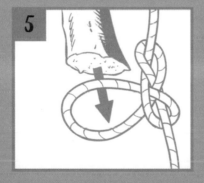

Push a length of branch
into the new loop. Tug
on the rope so the knot
takes shape and is tight.

6

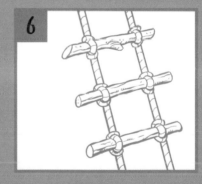

Repeat the knots at
intervals on this rope
and then the other one
to make a ladder.

HOW TO ...
SURVIVE A SHARK ATTACK

Unsurprisingly, the best way to survive a shark attack is to avoid sharks in the first place. While the danger of being attacked by a shark is hugely exaggerated in many movies (you are statistically more likely to be killed by a hippopotamus than a shark), swimming in shark-infested water isn't a smart thing to do. However, if you do find yourself among fishy friends, take these precautions to minimize your chances of becoming a shark snack.

When the shark attacks, don't freeze with fear. Hit it with a sharp object or your fists. Aim your blows at its eyes, gills or at the end of its nose, which are its most sensitive areas.

DOS AND DON'TS

- Sharks like to eat fish. Stay away from fishing boats and groups of sea birds where sharks are likely to be hunting.

- If you cut yourself, get out of the water immediately. Sharks can smell blood from a long way off and will soon come to investigate what is causing the delicious smell.

- Try to swim with a group of people. Sharks are less likely to attack if they are outnumbered. Also, the more people there are keeping an eye out for fins breaking the water, the safer you will be.

- Wear dark, plain colours. Brightly-coloured bathing costumes or wetsuits and even shiny watches and jewellery may catch the light and make you look like a tasty exotic fish.

- Never provoke a shark by lunging at it or waving your arms and legs around. If a shark feels threatened, it is much more likely to attack.

ACTION IF ATTACKED

If a shark has decided to attack, it will begin to dart to and fro, zig-zagging and lifting its head. Here's what to do:

- Swim away as quickly as you can and get out of the water. If you can't, stay calm. Don't thrash and splash about - the shark will think that you're injured and an easy kill.

- Try to get into a position where your back is protected by rocks, a reef, or by another swimmer. That way you can concentrate on defending yourself from the front.

HOW TO ...
SURVIVE A SWARM OF
ANGRY HONEYBEES

On its own, a honeybee is not particularly dangerous, but may sting you if it feels threatened. Honeybees die after they sting, so they avoid it if possible. But don't be fooled, multiple bee stings are dangerous and can be fatal. When bees swarm they can be very aggressive and will try to defend their hive at all costs. Here are some tips about what to do if you encounter a swarm.

DEALING WITH STINGS

1 A honeybee will leave its stinger in you once it has stung. Gently scrape this out with your fingernail as soon as you can to stop it injecting more venom.

2 Apply a cold compress to relieve the pain and swelling. Alternatively, apply a substance called 'meat tenderizer' (such as papain) to the area of the sting. This will break down the protein in the bee's venom. A paste of baking soda and water may also soothe the pain.

3 If you have been unlucky enough to receive more than a dozen stings, or have been stung in or around your mouth or nose, seek medical attention immediately.

GOOD IDEAS

- Put as much distance as you can between you and the hive. The bees will pursue and sting you until they no longer see you as a threat. Don't stand still, run!

- Take cover, in a building if possible, and shut all the doors and windows. If you can't, run through long grass or scrubland, which should give you some cover.

BAD IDEAS

- Don't approach a hive. Bees are territorial and more likely to attack if you go near their hive.

- Don't swat at the bees. It will make them sting you more because you are threatening their bee buddies.

- Don't attempt to escape by getting into water. They may wait above the water for you to surface.

WARNING

If you are allergic to bee venom and get stung, seek immediate medical attention.

SURVIVE A LONG CAR JOURNEY

When you're stuck in the back of the car on the way to visit your relations, boredom can strike at any time. Make sure you survive the trip.

THE NUMBER-PLATE GAME

This is a classic car-journey game, which can be played with any number of players. Simply start with the letter 'A' and take turns to look for number plates containing 'B', 'C', 'D' and so on. Although it's tempting, don't ask the driver to speed up simply for you to check out the number plate in front.

IN-CAR BINGO

Prepare a bingo sheet in advance for each person to work from. Offer a prize to the first person to spot all the items on their sheet. They may get to choose what music to play for the next half hour or decide where to stop for snacks next.

WHAT NOT TO DO

- Don't kick the back of the seat in front of you over and over again.

- Avoid singing the following song over and over again:
  'I know a song that'll get on your nerves,
  get on your nerves, get your nerves.
  I know a song that'll get on your nerves,
  here's how it goes . . .' (repeat)

- Resist asking any of the following questions:
  'Are we nearly there yet?'
  'Is it far now?'
  'When's lunch/dinner/breakfast?'

- Don't try to climb into the front seat from the back seat when the car is moving.

- Don't have a back-seat burping contest. However bored you are, it's in your best interests not to distract the driver from the road ahead.

HOW TO …

READ AN ORIENTEERING COMPASS

1 Hold the compass out flat so that the needle can spin around freely.

2 Stand still for a few moments until the north-seeking end of the needle (usually marked with red paint) settles in one position — this is magnetic north.

3 Keep the compass level and turn the dial until the orienting mark for north is on top of the coloured end of the needle. Now you know exactly which way south, east and west are, too.

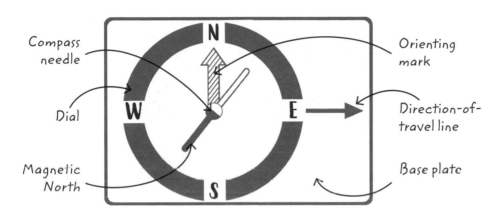

Compass needle — Dial — Magnetic North — Orienting mark — Direction-of-travel line — Base plate

Once you've learned how to read a compass you'll be able to use it to find your way even when there are no visible landmarks to take your bearings from. If you are out walking and want to set up camp that evening at the base of a hill in the distance, follow the instructions below.

1 Aim the compass so that the arrow indicating the direction-of-travel is pointing directly at the hill.

2 With the arrow still aimed at the hill, turn the dial until the orienting mark for north is on top of the north end of the compass needle.

3 Using these bearings you'll be able to follow the direction-of-travel line towards the hill, even if you have to walk through a forest — just walk towards the hill, keeping the needle firmly positioned on the mark for north.

HOW TO ...

COPE WITHOUT A COMPASS

If you are unfortunate enough to have forgotten your compass, all is not lost – as long as someone is wearing a wristwatch you'll be able to use the sun to work out which way is north.

The sun rises in the east and sets in the west wherever you are. However, did you know that at 12 noon in the northern hemisphere the sun is due south and at 12 noon in the southern hemisphere it is due north?

TOP TIP

If you only have a digital watch with you, simply draw a clock face on a piece of paper. Find out the time on your digital watch and mark where the hands would be on an analogue clock on your picture. Then follow the instructions on the next page.

NORTHERN HEMISPHERE

To find south in the northern hemisphere:

- Hold your watch horizontally and aim the hour hand directly at the sun.

- The point on the watch face between 12 o'clock and the hour hand is due south.

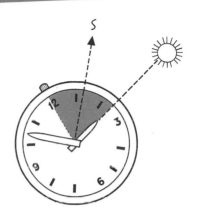

SOUTHERN HEMISPHERE

To find north in the southern hemisphere:

- Aim 12 o'clock on the watch face at the sun.

- Divide the angle between the hour hand and 12. This gives you the direction of north.

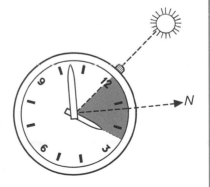

MAKE A COMPASS USING THE SUN

You can still work out roughly which direction is which, even without a compass or a watch, just by using the movement of the sun. You need a little bit of time to get this right. Don't forget, north and south are reversed in the southern hemisphere.

YOU WILL NEED:

- A long, straight stick
- Two medium-sized pebbles
- Some level ground
- A piece of string and a twig

1 Place the stick in the ground and mark the tip of the stick's shadow in the morning with one pebble.

2 Draw a semi-circular line around the stick (use a piece of string tied to the stick and a twig at the other end to mark the ground). The line should be the same distance away from the stick as the pebble.

3 The stick's shadow will get shorter as the time gets closer to 12 noon, and longer as the afternoon goes on. Wait until the stick's shadow touches the edge of the semi-circle again and mark the point with your second pebble.

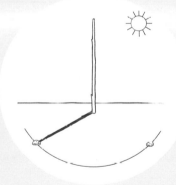

4 As the sun moves across the sky from east to west the shadow from the stick will move in the opposite direction, from west to east. The line between your morning pebble and your evening pebble marks a line from west to east, so if you draw another line at a right angle to this, you will also have north and south.

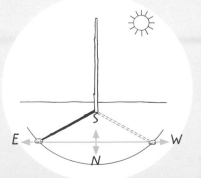

SURVIVE A HAUNTING

Whether or not you personally believe in ghosts, some people certainly do. They will swear that things happen in their houses that are hard to explain – objects move, there are strange noises, cold areas in rooms, or they even catch glimpses of the ghosts themselves.

Perhaps you feel fine or even excited about having a ghost in your house. This is useful when surviving a haunting because experts believe that making friends with a ghost is the best way to stop it doing annoying things around your house.

Talking to the ghost is a positive thing to do. Some say that ghosts are confused and unsure of why they are stuck on Earth. Try reminding the ghost that it has loved ones waiting for it 'on the other side'. This might spur it into moving on. Or you can try simply telling the ghost in a loud voice that you'd like it to leave. You never know, it might be a timid spirit who is easily spooked.

OUT, OUT, OUT!

If giving the ghost a good talking-to doesn't work, take a lit candle and a silver bell into every room in the house. Walk to each corner of each room with the candle in one hand and ring the bell with the other.

Next take the candle and the bell outside and visit each corner of the house, too. This supposedly has the effect of chasing the ghost out of any corner it has become comfortable in.

ANTI-SPOOK DEVICES

Other ways of deterring the house ghost include:

- Sprinkling a thin line of sea salt along each window sill and doorway

- Scattering rice on the kitchen floor overnight

- Painting your front door red

- Placing your shoes on the floor before you go to bed so that they point in different directions.

Try all these at once and the ghosts will probably leave your house and stay away for good — as will all your friends, who will think you are crazy ...

ESCAPE TRICKY SITUATIONS

You are mistaken for a spy and seized by undercover agents.
You are tied up with rope and bundled into the boot
of a car. Here's what you need to do:

THE ROPE ESCAPE

It is important to start your escape while being tied up. The trick
is to make your body take up as much space as possible. Draw your
arms into your body and hunch your shoulders. Breathe in deeply
and swell your chest out. Flex and expand your muscles as much as
possible. Hopefully this will mean that when you relax and breathe
out there is some slack in the rope. This will make your wriggle
to freedom much easier. If your wrists and ankles are being tied,
discreetly hold your arms and legs as far apart as you can while
they are being bound.

The rope escape is all about getting a feel for the rope. First wriggle
a little and try to feel where the ropes are loosening and try to poke
out an elbow or an arm. Once one of your arms is free you can begin
to work on the knots with your hand.

If your feet are tied, try to slip off your shoes, as this will make
getting free much easier.

THE CAR-BOOT ESCAPE

Car boots are hot and stuffy places, so it is essential to remain calm. Panicking will raise your heart rate, increase your body temperature, which makes the boot hotter, and increase your breathing, which uses up valuable oxygen. Focus your attention on escape and breathe slowly and regularly.

It sounds obvious, but look for a quick-release mechanism. Many cars have these installed. It would be located near the catch that keeps the boot closed, and rather helpfully, it may even glow in the dark.

If there is no quick release, look for a boot-release cable. Search under the carpet, or along the sides of the boot. When you find the cable, pull it to release the catch.

A car's tail lights can usually be accessed from inside the boot. You might have to remove a panel in the boot to get to them. Once you find the lights, try to push or kick out the unit. This will let in some air and create a space from which you can signal for help to passing cars and pedestrians.

WARNING

A car boot is hot, cramped and almost airtight, so there's not much oxygen on offer and you could suffocate. Do not ever, under any circumstances, shut yourself or anyone else in a car boot.

HOW TO ...
AVOID BEING ATTACKED BY A POLAR BEAR

Polar bears rarely attack humans, preferring a diet of seals and fish to human flesh. However, they're strong and very curious, so it is best to take precautions to avoid attack.

POLAR PRECAUTIONS

- Visit the South Pole not the North Pole. Polar bears only live in the Arctic Circle, so you'll be out of paws' reach.

- When possible, sleep in concrete buildings. Polar bears have claws that can grow up to 13 cm long, and will make short work of a tent. Male bears can weigh up to half a tonne and would flatten a wooden hut with ease.

- Polar bears have an excellent sense of smell. Always keep your camp clean and tidy. The smell of rubbish will attract hungry bears from far and wide.

- Stay away from dead animals you find on the ice. A bear may be near by looking for an easy meal and if he sees you he might prefer fresh meat.

If you do encounter a polar bear, never turn and run. Stand up in front of it holding your coat or a blanket over your head to make yourself look bigger than you are. Wave your arms around and make as much noise as possible.

With luck the bear will decide you are too difficult a meal to bother with and head off for a seal snack.

HOW TO ...
TICKLE A FISH

Tickling a fish, also known as 'noodling', is an old poachers' trick (a poacher is someone who unlawfully takes or kills fish or game). It is the art of taking a live fish from water with your bare hands.

WARNING

Unsurprisingly, tickling fish is illegal, so this is a survival skill that you should only use if you are stranded in the outdoors without any food.

1

Find a stream or river with a good flow of clear water that is no deeper than knee-high.

2

Walk slowly and quietly along the bank upstream (which means in the opposite direction to the current). Keep low, and look out for fish lying close to the bank, near weeds and under stones – in running water, stationary fish always face upstream, so that water can pass through their gills as they open and close their mouths, allowing them to breathe.

3

The fish are not always easy to spot. Stop and crouch down as soon as you see one – you don't want to scare the fish away. Choose a part of the river or stream where the sun isn't behind you, otherwise your shadow will fall on the water and spook any fish.

4

When you've found a fish close enough to your bank, stay just behind it, out of its sight. Then lie on the bank on your belly. Inch forward towards the edge until you are next to the fish, but don't thump on the bank — fish can feel the vibrations through the water.

5

Next, very slowly and gently, so as not to startle your slippery friend, move your hand and arm into the water until your hand is behind the fish's tail, on the side of the fish away from the bank.

6

Slowly move your hand forward until it is just beneath the fish's gills, and then bring it upwards until you are just touching the fish. Move your hand centimetre by centimetre, and immediately stop and let the fish settle if it shows signs of being disturbed.

7

Now, using a very light touch, slowly move your hand back along the fish's tummy, and continue to repeat this stroking gesture until the fish starts moving its tail and gills in glee and looking like it is mesmerized.

8

Now act with lightning speed. Quickly and firmly close your hand around the fish just behind the gills, and in the same movement flick it out of the water and on to the bank, far enough away from the edge that it can't wriggle back into the stream.

9

Since you want to eat your catch, take a firm hold of it and kill it at once by knocking it sharply on the top of the head — at a point just behind the eyes — with a stone or heavy stick.

GET RID OF LEECHES

The bad news is leeches are blood-sucking, slug-like creatures that lurk in damp places, such as rainforests, tropical jungles, marshes and swamps, just waiting to stick themselves on your skin and gorge themselves on your blood. The good news is that they are not usually harmful, but they can carry bacteria and viruses. Here's how to deal with the little suckers if you need to:

1 In places where leeches are plentiful, if you wade through water they will find you, and if you stand still for a few minutes, you'll see leeches dropping from vegetation and moving towards you. They are attracted by the sound you make and your scent. Use insect repellent on your skin and clothing. Cover as much of your skin as possible. Full armour is an option but you are in danger of sinking in boggy terrain!

2 When on an expedition, regularly check your skin to see if any leeches have attached themselves to you.

3 If you find a leech, locate the 'oral' sucker. This is at the thinner end of the leech. Slide a nail sideways underneath and scrape the leech off your skin gradually.

4 When the thin end of the leech has been unstuck, quickly slide your finger under the fat end to dislodge it, too. Watch out, the leech will try hard to reattach itself.

5 Carefully check the rest of your body for more leeches. You never know where they could be hiding.

6 Make sure any wounds on your skin caused by leeches stay clean — that way they have less chance of becoming infected.

LEECH DON'TS

- Never be tempted to wrench a leech off your body. Bits of its jaws might get left in your skin and cause an infection.

- Don't try to burn the leech off with a flame or tip salt over it. The leech might let go and fall off, but before it does it might spit the blood that it has sucked out back into your blood along with all sorts of nasty bacteria.

HOW TO ...

PUT SOMEONE IN THE RECOVERY POSITION

If you find a member of your expedition unconscious, immediately call for assistance from a qualified medic. If you suspect they have a neck or spine injury, do not attempt to move them unless they are in immediate danger. The recovery position is a first-aid technique that can be used on a teammate who is unconscious, but is still breathing normally and who doesn't have a neck or spinal injury.

BEFORE STARTING

Open the patient's mouth and make sure that their airway is clear of any blockages, including their tongue. Tilt their head back and raise their chin. Check that the patient is breathing normally by looking to see if their chest is moving up and down regularly, listening at their mouth and feeling the air on your cheek. Then check that their heart is still beating by feeling for their pulse. You are now ready to put the patient in the recovery position.

1 Gently lay the patient on their back. Kneel by their right-hand side. Take the arm nearest to you and lay it on the ground in a right angle.

2 Reach over and take the other hand and bring it across their chest. Bend the arm and place the back of the hand on the patient's cheek nearest to you, holding it there with your own hand.

3 Pull up the far (left) leg at their knee until the sole of their foot is on the ground. Then, gently bring the knee towards you (keeping your hand and the patient's against their cheek). As their left knee comes forward, your casualty should roll on to their right side.

4 Remove your hand from the patient's cheek making sure that their head is still resting on their own hand. Move the leg towards the chest to form a right angle.

5 Keep the airway open by tilting the patient's head back and raising their chin. Check their breathing and pulse.

6 Keep a close eye on your teammate until help arrives, and check their breathing regularly.

HOW TO ...
SURVIVE
AN AVALANCHE

Snow avalanches occur when the snow on a mountain slope becomes so heavy that all it wants to do is travel downhill. Over a million avalanches happen every year, so they're a serious hazard during an expedition in mountains.

AVOID THE DANGER

- Always make sure you carry a snow shovel and an avalanche rescue beacon. The beacon will send out a signal that rescuers can follow if you are buried in snow. Turn the beacon on when you set out on your expedition.

- Before crossing a slope, secure your snow goggles and put on your hat, gloves and a scarf. Zip up your coat and tighten the neck and cuffs. If an avalanche does happen, it will be harder for the snow to get inside your clothes.

- Choose one member of your team to make their way across the slope first. Then make sure everyone in your team crosses in the same track. Tell them to concentrate on the snow on the slope above them for any sign of movement.

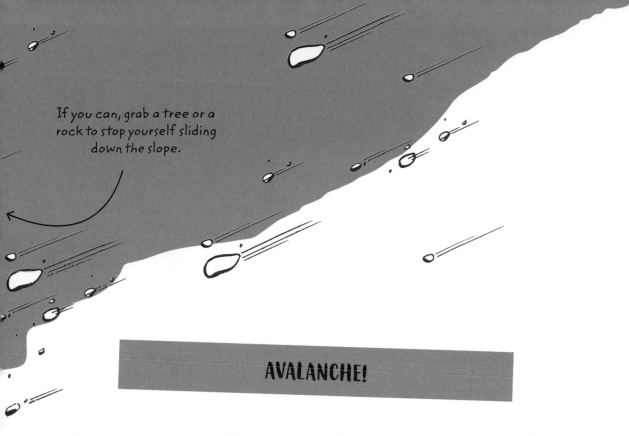

If you can, grab a tree or a rock to stop yourself sliding down the slope.

AVALANCHE!

Just before an avalanche hits, scream as loud as you can to warn the other members of your team, but when the snow reaches you, close your mouth so you don't swallow any.

Don't try to outrun or out-ski the avalanche — it can move at speeds of over 100 km per hour.

Avalanche snow is a bit like water. Once the snow has hit you and knocked you off your feet, try to swim through the snow. You can stay nearer the surface by swimming upwards, and this improves your chances of being rescued. As you come to a halt, curl up in a ball with your hands over your face while the snow covers you. Next, wiggle your head around in the snow to make a breathing space.

If you can see light, try to escape, or at least reach your hand above the surface where it can be seen. Don't waste valuable energy struggling if you aren't getting anywhere. Your avalanche beacon will be sending out signals giving your location, so remain calm and wait for help.

SURVIVE IN BEAR COUNTRY

Bears are as reluctant to bump into you as you are to bump into them. Unfortunately, they can't resist the smell of the food you have brought on your expedition. It's essential to do everything you can to avoid bears visiting your camp for lunch.

THE BEAR NECESSITIES

1 Never store food in your tent – keep it at least 50 m from camp in bear-proof boxes. Alternatively, store your food in an airtight container, put it in a bag, and hang it from the branch of a tree. Select a branch strong enough to support the bag but not a bear climbing along it.

2 Establish your cooking area at least 50 m from camp. Always clean up thoroughly after eating. Burn or bury all leftover food well away from camp. Dispose of all cooking or washing-up water away from camp, too.

3 Never keep scented items or toiletries in your tent. Toothpaste and lip-balms are tasty treats for bears.

4 Don't burn 'citronella' candles (sold to keep insects away). Their lemony scent has been known to attract bears.

5 Never put food out for bears in the hope you will spot one. They will only come closer and closer hoping for more food and might get angry when you can't give them any more.

6 When you are out and about, make plenty of noise. Any bears in the area will probably stay out of your way. Attach bells to your ankles or clap and sing as you hike. This is particularly important when other noises, such as running water, may hide the sound of your footsteps.

BEAR BEWARE

- If a bear approaches, don't turn and run or shout and scream. Speak in a calm voice and back away with your head tilted downwards (but keep your eyes on the bear).

- If a bear attacks you, play dead. Roll onto your front and curl into a ball clasping your hands behind your neck. Stay in this position until the bear loses interest. It might just be curious and want to play around with you for a bit. If it doesn't show signs of leaving you alone, or becomes more ferocious, fight it off with all your might.

HOW TO ...
BUILD A
SURVIVAL SHELTER

This easy survival shelter can be made in a couple of hours. It will keep you warm and dry, and will help you get a good night's sleep, which is vital in preserving your strength and maintaining a positive attitude. Here's how to build it:

1 Find two strong, straight sticks, each with a fork at one end. Make sure they are the same length (about 1.2 m). Sharpen the unforked ends and dig them firmly into the ground to a depth of at least 40 cm, and 2 m apart. If one stick is longer than the other, dig it further into the ground to even up the height.

2 Find another long, straight stick over 2 m long and rest this in the forks of the upright sticks. This is your 'ridge pole'. Secure it to the forked sticks with twine.

3 If you have a tarpaulin throw it over the ridge pole to make a tent. If it is large enough, use some of the tarpaulin to form a floor for you to make your bed on.

4 Peg the tarpaulin down with sticks, or place heavy stones along the wall edges to keep it secure.

AN ALTERNATIVE SHELTER

If you don't have a tarpaulin, make a shelter by building two walls out of branches and poles.

1. Find a long pole (about one and a half times as high as the tallest person using the shelter). Find a tree with a forked branch to support your shelter at one end.

2. Place the pole against the tree, then place smaller poles each side of the main pole to make a sloping framework.

Weave some thin, bendy branches through the small poles to make a criss-cross frame.

3. Cover your frame with materials such as dead leaves, dry ferns, moss and grass. Then spread a thick layer of dry grass on the floor of the shelter for you to lie on.

Add some light branches to the outside of the shelter to stop your insulating material blowing away.

HOW TO ...
SURVIVE A VISIT FROM AN ABOMINABLE SNOWMAN

Picture yourself trekking through the Himalayas in Tibet. There are many dangers you will have prepared for before setting out – the cold, snowy conditions, the treacherous, rocky landscape and the low oxygen levels that you will find at this high altitude. What you might have forgotten to prepare for, however, is a visit from an abominable snowman, known to his friends as a 'yeti'.

Some people don't actually believe that yetis exist, but, just in case you encounter one, here are some rules to follow:

1 Never enter into a long discussion with him or her about whether or not you believe in yetis. This is guaranteed to make a yeti very angry. Imagine if you had trekked across a wild and desolate landscape in search of food or company only to be told that you don't exist — wouldn't that make you abominably bad-tempered?

2 Don't run around screaming or throwing things at the yeti. Yetis are bigger and stronger than you and if you make them cross they may attack. Stay calm and slowly back away with your arms out in front of you, your hands clearly visible and palms downwards. This will put the yeti at ease and show him that you are not about to reach for something to throw at him.

3 Some people believe yetis are the distant cousins of human beings. So why not offer the yeti a cup of tea or some food? Snow people are often amazed by our abominable lack of manners when receiving guests. When a yeti has guests they will always offer some wild rhododendron tea and a few snow biscuits at the very least, even if the guest was not invited.

4 Don't flash cameras in a yeti's face — snow people find this very rude. Always ask the yeti's permission before taking their photograph so they have enough time to arrange their fur in a pleasing way. If you ask the yeti nicely enough they may even let you pose in the shot with them.

HOW TO ...
SEND AN
SOS

If you find yourself in need of rescuing, whether stranded on land or at sea, your priority is to attract the attention of potential rescuers. You need to send out an urgent signal for help called an 'SOS'. Here are some ways to do this:

FIRE, FIRE!

Fires are effective if they are built in a clearing. By day, the smoke can be seen from a distance. By night, the light from a fire will be visible from even further away. Three fires arranged in the shape of a triangle is a distress signal. Add leaves, fresh grass, ferns and damp wood to your fires to produce smoke, which will increase visibility during daylight. Use drier wood for a brighter blaze at night-time.

- Make sure there is nothing near by that can catch light if your signal fires flare up or blow out sparks, and don't build any fires in a dry or wooded area.

- When you have finished signalling, remember to put out your signal fires by covering them with soil or pouring water on them until all the embers have stopped glowing.

- Never signal for help unless you genuinely need it — you might spark a false rescue attempt.

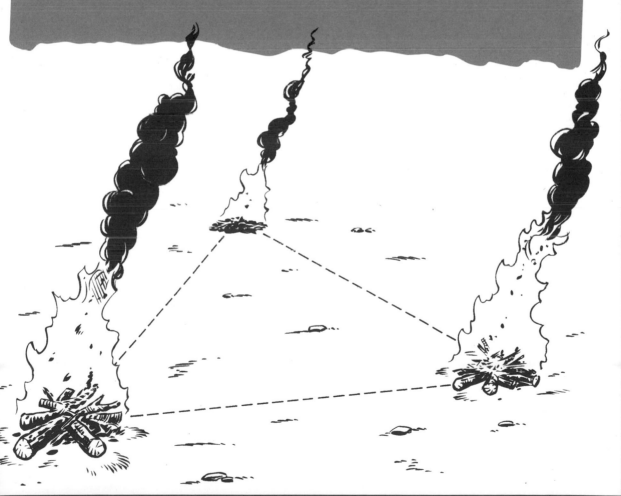

PLANE SPOTTER

To make sure you alert a passing helicopter or plane to your location, mark out a large signal on the ground that can be seen from the air. Reflective materials, such as metal wreckage from a car or plane, or any brightly coloured materials, are ideal. Use branches or stones if that's all you can find.

Arrange the objects so they spell out 'SOS', or form a geometric shape, such as a triangle or square. In nature, objects rarely form regular shapes so a search party is much more likely to notice an unnatural, man-made arrangement of objects.

GOT THE MESSAGE?

'Morse code' uses a combination of long and short pulses of light or sound to communicate letters and numbers. An SOS in Morse code can be sent using a torch. Alternatively use a shiny surface, such as a mirror or a polished piece of metal, to reflect sunlight. Direct your flashes of light towards the ship or aircraft you are trying to attract.

To send an SOS in Morse code, repeat this sequence:

Three short flashes, three longer flashes, three short flashes.

Stop signalling if you are certain that your signal has been seen — otherwise you might confuse your original SOS or dazzle the pilot of an aircraft.

When you are rescued, make sure any SOS signals that you have made on the ground are cleared away. That way nobody else will see them and think someone needs help.

HOW TO ...

BUILD AN IGLOO

1 Use a stick to mark a circle in the snow about 3.5 m across. Grab a snow shovel and dig out the circle to a depth of about 15 cm. Trample down the circle of snow with your feet.

2 Find a large, clear area of deep snow near by and jump on it until it is flat. This is going to be your snow quarry.

3 Use your shovel to cut out some snow bricks about 70 cm long, 50 cm wide and 20 cm deep.

4 Build a layer of snow bricks around the outside of your circle. Shape the bricks so that the row makes a spiral shape.

Leave a gap for the entrance.

5 Build a second layer of bricks, cutting each brick so that they continue to make a spiral. Then create more layers of bricks until you have an igloo shape with a hole at the top.

Get a friend to work from the inside of the igloo, filling in the cracks with snow.

6 'Cap' the hole with a single block of packed snow. Cut a block that is slightly bigger than the hole and get your partner to help lift it up to the top of the igloo and put it in place.

7 Climb inside the igloo and trim the cap so that it fits the hole. Pack snow around the edges of the cap.

8 Dig out a little trench from the snow leading up to the entrance hole.

9 Make an arch over your entrance hole by placing two narrow bricks either side. Make sure the arch will be big enough for you to crawl through easily.

10 Make a couple of small slits near the top and bottom of the igloo. These will allow air in and out.

WARNING

Keep your igloo-building skills for Arctic expeditions. Igloos can be dangerous if they collapse on top of you. So at home, stick to snuggling up in your own heated home. And if you must build an igloo in snowy territory, make sure you don't do it alone.

ESCAPE FROM QUICKSAND

Quicksand is a thick sludge that is most commonly found near beaches or rivers. In the movies people slowly sink into it, unable to escape, until their heads finally disappear beneath the surface and they're never seen again.

In reality, getting stuck in quicksand doesn't mean an inevitable death. It is often only half a metre deep and you'll stop sinking when your feet touch the solid bottom.

BE PREPARED

The most important thing is to be prepared and not to allow yourself to get stuck.

- If you are travelling in a team, spread out. Make sure you walk with a ten-pace gap between each team member. This way if one of you starts sinking the others can stop and help rather than take a sand bath with you.

- Use a stick to prod and test the ground in front of you.

- Carry a length of rope that you can use to lasso nearby objects and pull yourself clear in emergencies.

- Walk barefoot. The soles of shoes can act like a sink plunger, and will suck you down as you try to pull your feet out of quicksand.

Most people who perish in quicksand die by drowning. This is because quicksand is usually found in tidal areas. When the tide comes in, the area is submerged under water, as is anyone stuck in the sand.

ESCAPING A STICKY SITUATION

As soon as you feel you are sinking, throw away any heavy objects you are carrying, such as your rucksack or daypack. You must avoid allowing your feet to plunge down into the sand under the weight of your body. Quickly lean your whole body backwards until you are lying flat. This will spread out your weight and help you float on the surface of the sand.

Lie still. Don't thrash around. Any sudden movements will stir up the quicksand and make it less stable. Wait for the sand to settle around you. Carefully manoeuvre your walking stick underneath your hips, so you are lying across it. It will help keep you on the surface.

Stay on your back, but use your arms and legs to swim, crawl and drag yourself towards solid terrain. Move very slowly, edging your way to firmer ground.

Breathe in deeply and fill your lungs with air to increase your buoyancy.

HOW TO ...
TIE A QUICK-RELEASE KNOT

This quick-release knot is ideal for tying up something just for a little while, such as a hammock that you want to have a quick nap in. The knot will stay put, but if you tug on the loose end you can make it unravel.

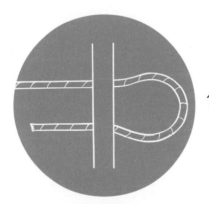

1 Put a loop round a post or tree.

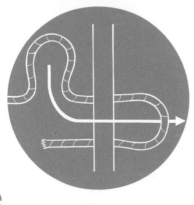

2 Make a kink and pass it through your loop.

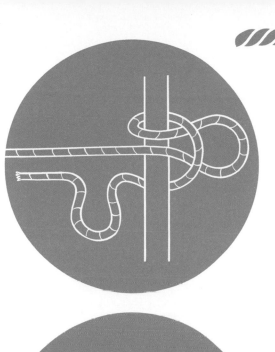

3 Make another kink from the lower end of the rope.

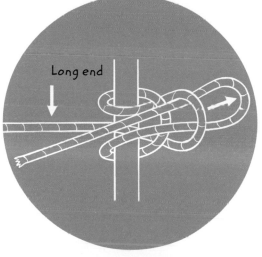

4 Pass this kink through the first kink. Pull on the long end of the rope to secure the knot.

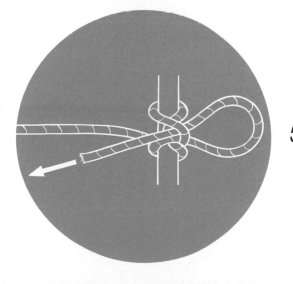

5 To release the knot, pull on the short end.

HOW TO ...
TRACK ANIMALS

Before you can track down a wild animal, you must be able to recognize its footprints. Memorize the animal tracks below, then read on for how to find your beast.

Here are some tracks you won't mind finding:

Dog   Cat   Fox   Badger   Running rabbit

Here are some tracks you should not follow:

Hyena   Bear   Hippo   Mountain lion

TRACKER TIPS

- The best time to go tracking is early in the morning or late in the day. When the sun is low in the sky, tracks will be edged with shadow, making them more visible.

- Always take a tracking guidebook with you, so you can identify any unusual tracks you come across.

- Scout around for tracks. Brush loose leaves and vegetation aside. If soil and vegetation appears worn down, look out for animal tracks, as these will be routes that animals take regularly.

- When you find a trail of prints, mark each one by pushing a stick into the ground next to it. This will help you to see the size of the animal's stride and guess at how big the animals might be.

- Use a magnifying glass to look closely at the prints. You might find an animal had a clipped hoof or damaged claw. This will help you distinguish it from other animals.

- Look out for droppings, chewed plants and any other signs of animal activity.

Don't look down at your feet. You'll track down the animal much faster if you look between 5 m and 10 m away from your body. Stay low, move slowly, and be as quiet as you can. Even the sound of a snapping twig could make your animal run off.

ON THE RIGHT TRACK

As you get closer to the animal you are tracking, its footprints will become cleaner, with less spare dirt, twigs and leaves lying on top of them. Its droppings, being fresher, will be warmer and softer. At this point, slow down in case you come across the animal and startle it.

If the wind is behind you, you might want to leave the trail and creep around the outside of the animal's tracks, so that your scent doesn't get blown towards the animal and scare it away.

If you need to hide, take refuge in a bush and get down on your hands and knees — failing that, lie down in some long grass and crawl along the ground using your arms.

MAKE A TRACKING STICK

Animal tracking is great fun, and this tracking stick will help you master the art.

1 Find a branch about a metre in length.

2 Use this to measure the distance between one footprint and the next footprint left by the same foot, from heel to heel. This will give you the length of the animal's stride. Use a sharp stone to scratch a mark on your stick in the position of each heel (X and Z).

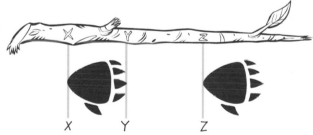

3 Hold the stick with point X at the heel of the first footprint and measure the length of this print. Use your stone to scratch a mark at the front of the print as point Y.

4 To begin using the stick, hold it so that point X is over the heel of the rearmost print and then look close to point Z for the next track. Repeat this process until you track down your animal.

HOW TO ...
SURVIVE BEING STUCK IN A LIFT

If you find yourself stuck in a lift, remain calm. You are not in a movie and a modern lift is very unlikely to come crashing down (even if the cables snap). Another thing modern lifts don't have is hatches in the ceiling through which you can escape. This would be pretty dumb and dangerous anyway.

1 Press each of the floor buttons one by one. Then try the 'door open' button. If none of these buttons work, the lift is broken and you need to let someone know about it.

2 If you can see light through any gap between the lift doors, the lift has probably stopped near a floor and it should be easy for you to shout for help and be released. The doors can be opened with a key. Don't try to force the doors open yourself. If the lift starts working when you are halfway out, you could be in for a nasty surprise.

3 If you can't see light through the doors, you have probably stopped between floors. Look for an emergency telephone. If there isn't one, look for an alarm button. Press this repeatedly. Someone should hear you and get help.

4 If you have waited for more than half an hour and nobody has arrived to help, shout and bang the inside walls of the lift with a set of keys or a shoe. If there are still people in the building, you need to get their help before they leave for the night.

5 If everyone has left the building and no one is responding to the alarm, the worst-case scenario is that you could be in the lift overnight. If this happens, there's no point panicking. Make yourself comfortable and get some sleep (and hope you don't need the loo).

SURVIVE AT THE SCHOOL DISCO

Picture the scene – something terrible is playing on the sound system, lights are flashing, your teachers are desperately trying to look cool, and you are surrounded by classmates. Classmates who want to dance with you.

If this situation is right up your street, select the person you want to dance with. Ask them confidently but nicely to dance. Whisk them onto the dance floor.

Whirl each other around (roughly time to the music will do) and thr... some serious shapes.

THINGS TO SAY

- 'I really like your hair style.'
- 'Do you dance professionally?'
- 'That colour really suits you.'

THINGS NOT TO SAY

- 'What's that in your hair?'
- 'Where's that smell coming from?'
- 'My friends dared me to ask you to dance.'

EVASIVE ACTION

If the very thought of dancing with your classmates sends shivers down your spine, you have two options. You can stay at home, watch TV, feed your goldfish and go to bed early. Alternatively, go to the disco, but bandage one leg or one arm heavily. Stand at the side of the room and look as though you would love to dance, but you simply can't.

TOP TIP

If you'd rather dance by yourself you'll need a strategy to keep your classmates at a distance. Fling your arms around wildly, get really into the music and sing along loudly. You'll find a wide circle opening up around you.

HOW TO ...
MAKE A CATAPULT

Catapults are great for firing small stones at tin
cans in your back garden or for scaring off ferocious
animals that may attack your camp in the wilderness.
Who knows, your handy little sling could even come
in useful for fending off invading aliens or zombies.

WARNING

Never fire your catapult at a human being.
They certainly won't thank you for it and there's
a serious risk of hurting them.

CATAPULT CONSTRUCTION

1. Find a strong, but flexible, forked branch (about 2.5 cm thick). An evenly Y-shaped branch works best.

2. Next you need some elastic. Pull a bit out of some old trousers — just be certain you don't want to wear them again. Alternatively, use a bit of the inner tube of a bike's tyre. This will be stronger and less likely to snap.

3. Find a strong, oblong piece of fabric, big enough to hold a large marshmallow. Leather or denim will work well. Thread your elastic through two holes in the fabric so that the pouch sits in the middle as shown opposite.

4. Tie an end of the elastic sling to each prong of your forked stick.

5. Hold your finished catapult at the base and place a small stone, a conker or a marshmallow in the fabric pouch.

6. Pull back on the sling until the elastic is fully stretched. Aim through the 'V' made by the two upper arms of the catapult. Then let go of the sling to fire the catapult.

You'll need to practise if you want to hit a tin can.

HOW TO ...
CARRY SOMEONE TO SAFETY

If someone in your expedition team has sprained their ankle but is still conscious and can hold themselves upright, you can make a stable seat with your hands simply by joining forces with another person.

WARNING

Do not lift anyone that may have a serious injury unless it is absolutely necessary. For example, if they face oncoming danger, such as a fire.

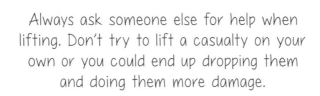

Always ask someone else for help when lifting. Don't try to lift a casualty on your own or you could end up dropping them and doing them more damage.

1 Following the picture shown below, place your right hand on your left wrist, and grip tightly. Ask your lifting partner to do the same.

2 Now grip their right wrist with your left hand and your left wrist with your right hand. Get them to do the same as you.

3 Lower the seat by both of you bending your legs, not your backs.

4 Get your casualty to sit on the four-handed seat and place his or her arms around both of the lifters' shoulders tightly.

5 When the casualty is seated, stand up, making sure you keep your back straight.

6 As soon as you have carried your casualty to safety find a trained medical person who can examine them.

HOW TO ...
MAKE AN UNDERWATER ESCAPE

You are deep in the mountains on a road trip, when suddenly the biggest, grizzliest bear lumbers in front of your windscreen. Your car swerves to avoid it and veers off the road, plunging into a nearby lake.

WARNING

Don't ever deliberately fill a car with water. You might drown accidentally and you certainly won't be able to ride to the cinema in it.

You are not doomed. Most cars will float for a while, giving you time to save the day. Immediately remove your seatbelt so you are ready for action.

As soon as your car enters the water, release the door locks. If you can, open the doors before the car begins to sink and use them to escape. You won't be able to open the doors once the car is partially submerged, because the weight of the water is pushing against them.

If the doors won't open, wind down your windows as quickly as possible. Electric windows should still work while your car is afloat, but will stop working as soon as the mechanism or the car's battery is submerged. Climb out of a window and swim to safety.

If you are unable to open your doors or windows, try to smash a window. Use something heavy such as a wrench or the metal end of a headrest, to smash at the corner of the window as this is where it is weakest.

If the car sinks before you can do any of the above, you are going to have to wait until the car has filled with water. This will equalize the pressure of the water inside and outside the car. Climb into the back seat because the front of the car, where the heavy engine is, will sink first. Wait until the water has reached neck height and take a big gulp of air. Once the doors are completely submerged, they should open with a push. Exit the car, and swim away and up to the surface.

HOW TO ...
AVOID A
HUNGRY HIPPO

You're on an African safari when, out of nowhere, a 2-tonne hungry hippo appears. Hippos can spend up to 16 hours a day chilling out in water, but don't be fooled. They are extremely aggressive, fiercely territorial and very fast. A hippo can run at speeds of up to 48 kilometres an hour and can do so for over 100 metres before it needs to rest.

In short, there's not a great deal you can do to defend yourself against a hippo attack, so your best policy is to avoid one.

- If you encounter a hippo on dry land, don't startle it, walk away as quietly and quickly as possible.

- Never get between a mother hippo and her baby. Female hippos are extremely protective of their young.

- Don't sail down an African river where hippos can be found. Hippos attack people who disturb them when they are having a soak. They can hold their breath under water for five minutes, so just because you can't see a hippo, it doesn't mean that the coast is clear.

Never jump in the water to swim with a hippo. Bathing like a hippo might look like fun, but you aren't a hippo and there's no way you'll fool the hippo into thinking that you are — no matter how good you are at holding your breath.

TIE A SLING

1 Find a large piece of clean fabric, about a metre square. A pillowcase cut open into a square is ideal. Fold the fabric in half diagonally to make a triangle-shaped bandage.

2 Hold the bandage under the casualty's injured arm, placing one end over the opposite shoulder.

3 Bring the other end of the bandage up over the arm, and over the other shoulder.

4 Tie the two ends together at the back of the casualty's neck, making sure the arm is held gently but securely in place.

5 Use a safety pin to fasten the remaining corner of the bandage. Pin the corner to the sling near the elbow.

You might need to practise tying your sling a few times before you get it right, so find a willing friend — if they can sit still long enough.

HOW TO ...
SURVIVE
AN ESSAY CRISIS

Help! Your essay is due in the morning and you have been playing computer games all evening. Here's how to save your skin by whipping up an excellent essay in no time.

1. Think carefully about what you want to say. Scribble down some ideas to make a spider diagram. Then join up any ideas that are linked.

2. Organize your ideas on a big piece of paper. If you are presenting some information, divide it into categories. For example, if your subject is the history of exploration, you could have 'The First Explorers', 'Exploration Today' and 'What Is There Left To Discover?' Jot them down as headings, leaving plenty of space between them.

3. List the main points that should go under each heading. List any facts that back it up beside each point.

4. Write an introduction. It might seem odd not to start by writing an introduction, but now is a good time because you know what is in the essay. Just give a brief summary of your essay — don't explain what you have found out though — that's the job of the conclusion.

5. Write your conclusion last. If you have presented an argument (such as 'Why I should lead a team to the North Pole'), round it off by summarizing the main points of the argument that you have already mentioned. For example: 'I would be the youngest explorer to make the journey. As a result people would give me lots of money to finance the trip. I would look really cool in the newspapers pictured standing at the Pole.'

6. Hand in your essay with a proud grin and wait for your teacher to give you top marks.

SURVIVE A SNAKE BITE

Not all snakes are poisonous and even poisonous snakes don't always inject venom into a victim when they bite. However, always assume a snake is poisonous, just in case.

In the movies, the hero usually cuts across their buddy's snake bite with a knife and sucks out the poison. Don't do this. You might make yourself sick, and cutting the flesh around the bite might help the venom to spread and could cause infection.

Get to a hospital as fast as you can. Even if you don't immediately feel unwell, it is essential that you get medical treatment as quickly as possible. If the bite starts to swell up and changes colour, it means the snake that bit you was probably poisonous.

Make a note of the exact time of the bite and of the size and appearance of the snake. This information will help the doctors who treat the bite. If possible, telephone the hospital with these details before you get there – that way they can have the correct treatment ready when you arrive.

TOP TIP

If you can't get medical attention immediately, remain calm. Panicking will increase your heart rate and this will help the venom to spread throughout your body faster.

PRECAUTIONS

- If you've been bitten on your arm or hand, remove your watch as your hand or wrist might swell up and your watch could become painfully stuck. Remove any other pieces of tight clothing or jewellery that are near the bite.

- Dress the wound with a bandage that fits snugly, but not too tightly. You want to restrict the flow of blood slighlly to the bitten area, but not cut off the blood supply altogether.

- If you're with another member of your expedition party get them to wash your bite with soap and waler. Lie down flat so that the area of your body that was bitten is not higher than your heart. This will slow down the speed at which venom travels to this vital part of your body.

Tie a splint to the affected limb. This will restrict its movement and help prevent the venom from moving around the body.

AVOID PIRANHAS

If you find yourself on an expedition in a South American rainforest and you have no choice but to cross a river, spare a thought for piranhas.

You've heard of these ferocious fish with razor-sharp teeth who have a frightening reputation for stripping the flesh off animals, right down to their bare bones. Here are some tips for keeping the flesh on your bones where it belongs:

PIRANHA POINTERS

- Throw a dead animal, such as a goat or sheep, into the water downstream from where you want to cross. The carcass will attract the piranhas and give you some time to cross, but not much. If the shoal is big and hungry enough, it will demolish a dead goat in a few minutes and you will be next on the menu.

- Piranhas live in warm waters that are still or flow slowly. Make sure the point at which you attempt to cross the river is one where the water is cold or fast moving.

- Wait until dark before attempting to cross as this is when piranhas are least active. Then swim or wade smoothly through the water, keeping any splashing to a minimum so as not to alert the piranhas to your presence.

Piranhas can grow up to 50 cm in length, so they are not ideal swimming companions!

DON'T PANIC

Piranhas don't go out of their way to attack humans unless they are really hungry. They are most dangerous during dry seasons, when water levels are low and food is hard to come by. So you might want to set up camp and wait until another time of year to get across that river!

HOW TO ...
AVOID BEING ATTACKED BY A MAN-EATING TIGER

Tigers don't usually attack and eat humans unless they are old or injured and unable to hunt for other food. However, in some rare cases, a single tiger that has turned into a 'man-eater' has been known to kill dozens or even hundreds of people.

You find out that a man-eating tiger is on the loose in your vicinity, and may find its way to your camp, town or village. Follow the steps on the next page to prepare for and deal with the danger.

1   Make a papier-mâché face mask. Wear it on the back of your head, not your face, so you look as if you have two faces — one at the front and one at the back. A tiger doesn't like to jump on its prey from the front so your mask will confuse it.

2   Carry a club over your right shoulder at all times. Tigers attack humans on the back of their neck so you will be ready to defend yourself.

3   If you catch sight of the tiger just before it pounces, turn to face it and look it right in the eye.

4   If you see the tiger in the distance, make a run for it. Tigers won't try to chase you over long distances. If a tiger thinks you have already seen it and you are quite far away, it might just leave you alone and wait for another piece of meat to come along.

Tigers are excellent swimmers, so it will soon catch up with you if you leap into the village pond.

HOW TO ...
PREDICT RAIN

Knowing whether or not it is going to rain is an invaluable skill when leading an expedition. Rain can make surfaces dangerous and your team's progress slow, plus your friends will appreciate staying dry!

Sometimes all you need to do is take a quick look at your teammates' hair to judge whether the weather is about to change. This is because some curly-headed folk will find their hair curls up more tightly before it rains.

Alternatively, most flowers are quick to open up when rain threatens. Regularly check the air to tell if the scent of any near by blooms has become noticeably stronger.

Stay alert to unusual animal behaviour, too. Animals are often aware of differences in air pressure, which indicate a change in the weather. If you notice that buzzing insects have suddenly gone quiet or that birds have returned to the trees, it's probably a sign that you're about to get drenched and it's time for you to seek shelter as well.

CLOUD READING

Grey clouds in the sky don't necessarily mean that a heavy shower is brewing, but the skies can give you essential information about the weather. Check the following:

TIME OF DAY

A grey morning sky can actually be a sign of a glorious day to come, but if the sky turns grey and clouds over later in the afternoon it means rain is probable.

SHAPE

Thin and wispy clouds that are spaced far apart signal fine weather. When they gather together and get ominously larger, they are likely to produce rain quite suddenly.

HEIGHT

As a general rule, the higher a cloud is in the sky, the better the weather will be. A covering of low, dark cloud is usually bad news, suggesting a lengthy downpour is probably on the way.

COLOUR

Clouds that are dark underneath and very tall usually mean that thunder, lightning, hail and strong winds are plotting to wreak havoc.

HOW TO ...
SURVIVE A
ZOMBIE INVASION

A zombie attack is probably the hardest challenge you will face. Zombies (or the 'undead', as they prefer to be known) are notoriously difficult to kill because they are not actually alive. As soon as you hear reports of zombies in your area, follow this plan of action:

GAME PLAN

- Gather as many survivors of the invasion as you can — there is safety in numbers. Find yourselves a secure building to use as a base. Ideally it should be on high ground. This will offer an excellent vantage point from which you can spot zombie hordes approaching, and the undead can't climb because their knees don't bend. Stock up on plenty of food and water — you may be surrounded by the undead for days.

- Make sure the building has only two entrances (you need a second exit to escape through if zombies break through the front entrance). Build a barricade at each entrance and seal any other doors and windows with heavy furniture.

HOW TO SPOT A ZOMBIE

The living dead are easy to spot because, as their name suggests, they are dead people whose bodies have come alive again.

Look out for:

- Staring eyes

- Green skin

- A pungent smell of rotting and decay

- Slow stumbling walk, with arms held straight out in front and a limp caused by their stiff knees.

If survivors come to your base asking for shelter — beware. They may have been infected. This happens if they are bitten or scratched by a zombie. There is no cure. They will become zombies too. Check all newcomers for any wounds.

If someone has been infected you must get them out of your safe house quickly. The good news is once they are a full-blown zombie they won't feel pain and they'll never be forced to do anything they don't want to again, such as be nice to their granny. The bad news is they'll stink and their flesh will fall off.

BATTLING WITH THE UNDEAD

After a while you may get bored of waiting it out in a barricaded base. Television broadcasts will eventually stop and there'll be nothing but the sound of static on the radio. You may decide to venture outside. Be very careful. Whenever you leave the shelter to gather fresh supplies or check for more survivors, carry a bat or sword to defend yourself. Guns are useless against zombies. You can knock a zombie's head off though, and stop it in its tracks.

BLENDING IN

If you find yourself caught in a crowd of the undead, your best chance of surviving is to act like a zombie. Moan and keep your eyes as wide open as possible. Limp and dribble. Zombies are pretty stupid and with any luck they won't notice you among them.

HOW TO ...
MAKE FRESH WATER FROM SEA WATER

If you are marooned on a desert island after a shipwreck, you'll be surrounded by water. Annoyingly, you won't be able to drink any of it because it is salty. With any luck, you'll have salvaged some useful utensils, such as cooking pots and tin cans, from the wreck of the ship. Using these, here's how to make delicious fresh water from nasty brine:

1. Stand a clean, empty tin can on the bottom of an empty cooking pot or bowl. Pop a stone into the can to keep it in place.

2. Pour sea water into the pot until the level is about three quarters the height of the can. Make sure the sea water does not enter the can.

3. Put the pot's lid on upside-down, so that the lid handle is over the empty can inside. Put the pot over a campfire and wait for the water to boil.

4. As the water boils, carefully pour a little cold sea water over the lid of the pot to keep it cool. Make sure that your fire doesn't go out. As the water boils it turns to steam and leaves the salt particles behind in the pan. The steam collects on the inside of the lid and, as it cools, 'condenses' into pure water droplets. The condensation then runs down the lid's handle, dripping into the can. Keeping the outside of the lid cool with cold water makes the steam condense faster.

5. After 20 minutes use some twigs as tongs to lift the lid of the pot and check the water's progress. Once the can is almost full, very carefully remove it from the pot with the tongs. The pot, can and water will be very hot.

6. Leave the can of water to cool before drinking.

WARNING

Don't try doing this unless you have been shipwrecked. Sea water tastes disgusting and is extremely bad for you if it has not been boiled in the correct way because it contains huge amounts of salt.

LIGHT A FIRE

There are several ways of making fire if you don't have any matches or a lighter. The 'fire-bow drill' is a clever version of the 'rubbing two sticks together' method. Follow the steps on the next page to do it.

SURVIVAL SKILL WARNINGS

It is extremely dangerous to start a fire. Always follow the advice below when starting a fire in a survival situation:

- Keep a container of water or soil at hand in case you need to put out your fire quickly.

- Choose a suitable spot for your fire, away from anything that could catch alight, such as trees, bushes, dry grass and buildings.

- Make sure that all your belongings are right out of the way and remove any stones from the area — they could get really hot and shatter.

- Always keep an eye on the fire to make sure it does not get out of control. When you have finished, make sure you put the fire out and that no embers are left glowing.

1   Collect some 'tinder'. Tinder is anything that catches fire very easily, such as dry, thin grass, cotton fluff and feathers. You need a good handful to start your fire.

2   Find a wooden stick for your bow. It needs to be a strong stick that is about 60 cm long and about 1 cm wide. It must be quite stiff, but still bendable. A thin bamboo cane is good for this.

3   Now you need some cord or string. A bootlace is perfect if it is long enough. Carefully carve a slight notch around each end of the bow. Attach the cord to the bow at either end around the notches. The cord should be stretched tightly enough to make the bow bend slightly.

4   The drill should be a piece of hard, dry branch about 30 cm long and 2.5 cm wide. It should have a sharp point at one end and be rounded and blunt at the other. The straighter your drill, the easier it will be to use. Twist the drill into your cord (see the picture on the next page).

5   Make a base called a 'fireboard'. You will need a flat piece of soft, dry wood, 2.5 cm thick, 15 cm wide and 60 cm long.

6   Carve a v-shaped notch in one end of the board about 2 cm deep and 2 cm wide, as shown overleaf. Put your tinder in the notch.

7 Make a hole in the board that is about the same width as your drill and 1.5 cm deep. The hole should be centred near the notch you made.

8 Find a stone with a natural hollow in it, about the same size as the blunt end of your fire drill. Push the blunt end of your drill in the stone's hollow and rest the sharp end in the hole on your board. Alternatively, make a hole in a piece of hardwood that fits in your hand and use that instead of the stone.

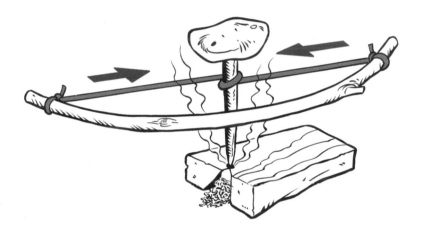

9 Kneel on one knee and place your other foot firmly on the fireboard. Push down lightly on the stone with one hand and hold the bow in your other. Pull the bow back and forth. Begin slowly, and keep a steady pace. Spin the drill until wood dust and smoke start to come out of the hole.

10 When you see smoke coming out of the hole, push and pull the bow faster and harder. The wood dust will fall into your notch and onto your tinder. When smoke starts to come from your pile of tinder, you have made a 'coal'. Gently blow on the smoke to produce a flame.

11 Now you have a little fire, you can add some small sticks, followed by some bigger ones until your flame looks stronger. You can then build your campfire around it using larger pieces of wood.

Hold your bow horizontally and your drill vertically. A pinch of sand in the hole under the drill will create more friction, and therefore more heat.

If there are two of you, take it in turns to blow, so that your wood powder doesn't cool down while you are taking a breather.

HOW TO ...
WADE THROUGH
RUNNING WATER

Wading through water – especially fast-flowing water –
can be very dangerous. So the rule is: never wade unless
you absolutely have to – for example, you are being
chased by a water-hating wild animal and you simply
can't get around the water, there's no bridge or
boat, and you've no means of building a raft.

PICK YOUR SPOT

- Make time to look at the stretch of water you're planning to cross, and, if there's time, find out us much about it as possible. How deep is it? How fast is the current? Are there any obvious shallows, sandbanks, islands, low overhanging tree branches or large rocks that might help you cross?

- Choose the best crossing site you can. Look for the area with the shallowest water and the gentlest current. Current travels faster on the outside of a river bend than on the inside, so avoid outside bends. It is very tricky to tell how strong the current is just by looking at the surface of the water – however, the shallower the water, the less force the current will exert on you as you wade. The pressure of fast-flowing water on your legs will come as a shock at first and it will increase as you edge deeper into the water.

- Look for a stretch of river where the banks are low. That way it will be easier to get in and out of the water.

- Very cold water can be extremely dangerous, as it will affect your body's ability to function. Never attempt to wade through water that is too cold.

1 Make a 'wading staff'. This should be a strong, straight stick, cut to about the height of your shoulder. If possible, make a wrist-loop from string or cord and lash it to the staff about 20 cm from the upper end. This will stop the staff getting lost if you drop it.

2 Take your trousers off, but keep your boots on. You will need them to grip the riverbed and they will protect your feet from anything sharp underwater.

3 Undo the belt of your backpack so that you can remove it quickly if you lose your footing while crossing.

4 Try to keep your belongings dry. Make a raft for your clothes and kit from a waterproof sheet. Put a bundle of sticks and some straw in the centre of your sheet (to create some air pockets), pile your trousers and clothes on top, then tie up the bundle with cord. Attach it to your belt. When the time comes, carefully float the bundle in front of you as you wade across.

5 Use your wading staff to test the riverbed and the depth of the water ahead of you. Even shallow places may have deep potholes, and there are often unseen obstacles, such as hidden rocks or waterlogged branches, or sudden patches of sticky mud or sand. The staff will also help you to keep your balance.

6 Aim to take a route that will take you across the river diagonally upstream, to another low bank. Face upstream and turn your body so that you are moving your feet sideways across the river. Shuffle your feet under water, one step at a time, using the staff to help you stay upright.

7 If you lose your footing don't panic. Lie on your back and let the current take you, feet first, downstream, using your hands as paddles to guide you into shallow water where you can stand up again.

WARNING

Wading through water is a skill that should not be used when your street floods. In everyday life you should never wade through water that is higher than your ankles. Stick to wading through your bath water. You know how deep it is in there.

HOW TO ...

MAKE A DUG-OUT CANOE

One day you stumble across a big fallen tree in your garden. Why not suggest your family works together to make a dug-out canoe from the tree, by digging out the wood from the tree trunk? You can demonstrate your amazing survival know-how and test your skill of matching different people to different tasks. You will gain serious credibility.

CHOP, CHOP!

1. Cut the branches from the fallen tree. Give this job to a big, strong, grown-up family member. Then ask them to saw off the length of trunk that will form your canoe.

2. Next, select someone to remove all the bark from the trunk.

3. When the trunk is bare, look carefully at how it is shaped and decide which end will be the slightly pointy front of the canoe called the 'prow'. Before turning the trunk over to begin digging out the wood, you need someone to shape the prow. It needs to form a gentle point that will cut through the water when you are paddling.

4. Next, get all your family members to work together to gently turn the trunk over. Wedge it firmly, to stop it rolling.

5. Before you begin digging out the interior of the canoe, mark out where the sides will be by scratching some marks in the wood. That way your team will only chop out wood that is inside that mark. If everyone works steadily for several days, the inside of the canoe will begin to appear.

6. Collect the chopped-out wood and put it in a safe place so it can be used as firewood.

7. As the wood is chopped out, the inside surfaces should be carefully shaped and smoothed so the sides are the same thickness all the way round.

FINISHING TOUCHES

When work has finished on the inside, roll the canoe over together and finish shaping the outside, chopping away any lumps to cut down the weight of your canoe. Use sandpaper to smooth the surface so it will glide through the water.

The last job is to make the canoe waterproof both inside and out. Some dug-out canoe-makers use boiled tree resin, which they spread over the wood. However, there are boat-building oils and varnishes that will do the same job and are much easier to use. Waterproof the canoe all over.

You will all be itching to try out the canoe on some water as soon as the last waterproof layer is brushed on, but it is up to you to make everyone wait until the canoe is completely dry inside and out.

Don't let anyone be too ambitious on the first outing and set off on a trip abroad. Plan a short trip in calm waters. Dug-out canoes need to be paddled gently.

If the canoe feels a bit wobbly when everyone is inside, you can fit small supports called 'outriggers' either side. These are hollowed-out lengths of wood, attached to the canoe by poles. When these are fitted securely, they will balance the canoe and reduce the chance of it tipping over.

Finally, you'll need paddles and floats. A cushion each will give members of your family something comfortable to kneel on while they are paddling.

Bon Voyage!

SOME EXCELLENT ADVICE

- Be careful how your family chops out the wood. If they cut too close to the edge of the tree trunk they could weaken the side or bottom of your canoe, or worse still, put a hole right through it.

- Ask them to cut notches across the trunk so that the chunks of wood between them can be chopped out more easily.

- Remain patient at all times. Making a dug-out canoe will take a long time, but it will all be worth it when the family can paddle their canoe down the river.

WARNING

Never try to make a dug-out canoe by yourself.
For one thing it will take you about a year, and for another thing, you run the risk of chopping up your finger instead of chopping up the tree trunk.

HOW TO ...

BE A MODEST HERO

Display heroic behaviour at all times,
but always be modest.

- Actions speak louder than words. Always do your fair share of the really unpopular tasks so that everyone can see you are prepared to pull your weight.

- Give your seat to older people on buses or trains — it shows you are both kind and considerate. Help an elderly person safely across the road whenever you can (but only when you're sure they want to be on the other side).

- Never boast. True heroes are quiet and unassuming. Play down all your achievements. If other people want to sing your praises, just shrug or shake your head as if you are embarrassed by the attention.

- No matter how much your arm hurts after falling out of a tree (having saved a kitten from certain death), brush aside offers of help or sympathy. Say things like "It's nothing", or "I'm used to this kind of pain". Cry later when you get home — your mum won't tell anyone. You'll always be a hero to her.

SURVIVE YOUR TEACHERS

School survival skills are among the most important skills you will learn in this book.

TEACHER TYPES

There are many types of teacher. Some think they are too cool for school and wear wacky waistcoats, and others, who know there is something you would much rather be doing, give you a mega-impossible project to do anyway. You suspect they would prefer it if you handed in the work late so they get to tell you off.

TEACHER'S PET

It doesn't matter what your teachers are like, the following tips will keep you in everyone's good books.

- **BE ON TIME.** This sounds boring, but teachers hate it when you are late and will use it as an excuse to pick on you for the rest of the day. Getting in early means you won't be put on the spot later when you might not have been paying attention.

- **REMEMBER THE EXCUSES THAT WORK.** If you hear your teacher shouting at a friend because they claimed the dog ate their homework, don't use that one yourself (even if it did). Make your excuses long and complicated. Hopefully your teacher will be bored by the time you get to the end, or even better stop you halfway through and just tell you to bring in your homework tomorrow.

- **SHOW SOME ENTHUSIASM.** Teachers find this encouraging and it makes the lesson go much quicker. Ask intelligent questions or request help when you need it. This shows that you want to learn and that you're not just sitting there waiting to go home.

- **EVERYONE GETS CAUGHT TALKING IN CLASS AT SOME POINT.** If this happens to you, you need to think quickly about what you were supposed to have been studying and claim that you were talking about that. Taking time to look up a relevant subject at the beginning of the class can save you detention time later.

CONGRATULATIONS

This is to certify that

....

is now a

BUSTER KNOW-HOW EXPERT